THINK YOUR WAY TO WEALTH

T0143882

Also available in the Condensed Classics Library

THINK YOUR
WAY TO WEALTH

by Napoleon Hill

*The Classic on Raising Your
Own Salary—Now Condensed*

Abridged and Introduced
by Mitch Horowitz

THE CONDENSED CLASSICS LIBRARY™

Published by Gildan Media LLC
aka G&D Media.
www.GandDmedia.com

Think Your Way to Wealth was originally published in 1948
G&D Media Condensed Classics edition published 2019
Abridgement and Introduction copyright © 2019 by Mitch
Horowitz

FIRST PRINT AND EBOOK EDITION: 2019

Cover design by David Rheinhardt of Pyrographx

Interior design by Meghan Day Healey of Story Horse, LLC.

ISBN: 978-1-7225-0213-3

Contents

An Old Classic Made New
By Mitch Horowitz

This book is written as a dialogue between success author Napoleon Hill and industrialist Andrew Carnegie. Hill said that he met the steel magnate for an interview in 1908, and that Carnegie pressed on him the idea of studying the principles of success and achievement found in the lives of great financiers, inventors, and high-achievers of all types. *Think Your Way to Wealth* is Hill's reproduction of that original dialogue.

The structure and language of the book are Hill's own. Written more than a decade after the appearance of his 1937 classic *Think and Grow Rich*, *Think Your Way to Wealth* gave Hill the opportunity to expand on some of the themes in his earlier book, and to call out ideas that he had omitted, such as the application of the Golden Rule and the use of what Hill called Cosmic Habit Force. Cosmic Habit Force is explored in the final and most powerful chapter of this book.

Think Your Way to Wealth is something of a personal milestone for me. It was the first audiobook that I narrated when I collaborated on its full-length recording in 2011. I can tell you from personal experience that you are fortunate to be encountering this abridgement. Although filled with sound and actionable ideas, Hill's original version of *Think Your Way to Wealth*, first published in 1948 (and sometimes alternately called *How to Raise Your Own Salary*), is one of his most verbose and drawn-out books. The original is uncharacteristically burdened with excess verbiage and repetition. It was probably written quickly and rushed to market. In this abridgment, I have tried to carve away the superfluous language to bring you the book's central ideas.

You will find in this abbreviated work not only a summation of Hill's best insights but a key articulation of his most important idea, which forms the foundation of his entire program: the possession of a Definite Chief Aim. If you take just one lesson from Hill's work, make it that one. You'll see why from experiencing the Hill-Carnegie dialogue in this book.

Like many lovers of Hill's work, I find that no matter how many times I experience his writings, I always find some new insight or emphasis, which refreshes my personal efforts. In this condensed edition of *Think Your Way to Wealth* I know you will discover or rediscover ideas that will lift your energies and drive you to new plans and strivings.

CHAPTER 1

Definiteness of Purpose

NAPOLEON HILL: Mr. Carnegie, please go back to the beginning of your career and describe your principles of achievement.

ANDREW CARNEGIE: To begin with, there are seventeen major principles of success, and everyone who attains his objective must use some combination of these principles.

The first is the most important. You may call it the Principle of Definiteness of Purpose. Study anyone who is a permanent success, and you will find that he has a definite major goal. He has a plan for the attainment of this goal. He devotes the major portion of his thoughts and his efforts to the attainment of this one purpose.

My own major purpose is that of making and marketing steel. I conceived that purpose while working as a laborer. It became an obsession with me. I took it to bed with me at night, I took it to work with me in the morning. My Definite Purpose became more than a mere wish; it became my burning desire. That is the only sort of definite purpose that brings results.

I must emphasize the vast difference between a mere wish and a burning desire that has assumed the proportions of an obsession. Everyone wishes for the better things of life but most never go beyond the wishing stage. Men who know exactly what they want of life, however, and are determined to get it, do not stop with wishing. They intensify their wishes into a burning desire and back that desire with continuous effort based on a sound plan.

It is necessary that they induce other people to cooperate in carrying out their plan. No great achievement is possible without the aide of other minds.

HILL: How long does it require, Mr. Carnegie, for one's mental attitude to begin attracting the physical and financial requisites of one's major purpose?

CARNEGIE: That depends entirely upon the nature and extent of one's desires and the control one exercises over his mind in keeping it free from fear and doubt and self-imposed limitations. This sort of control comes through constant vigilance, wherein one keeps his mind free of all negative thoughts and leaves it open for the influx and the guidance of infinite intelligence.

HILL: Do you follow the habit of writing down your major purpose, Mr. Carnegie?

CARNEGIE: I followed that habit many years ago, while I was struggling to make the change from day labor to industrial management. Moreover, I went much farther than merely reading my written statement of my major purpose. I met with my Mastermind group nightly, and we entered into a detailed roundtable discussion for the purpose of building plans to carry out the object of my major goal. I heartily recommend this roundtable habit.*

HILL: Why do you place a Definite Chief Aim at the head of the list of the 17 Principles of Achievement?

CARNEGIE: No one may achieve success without first knowing precisely what he wants. About 98 out of every 100 people are totally without a major goal, and it is

---

* You can learn more about this step in the following chapter and in *The Power of the Master Mind* by Mitch Horowitz (G&D Media).

significant that approximately the same percentage of people are considered failures.

HILL: Give me your definition of the word success.

CARNEGIE: My definition of success is this: the power with which to acquire whatever one demands of life without violating the rights of others.

HILL: Well, is it not true that success is often the result of luck?

CARNEGIE: If you will analyze my definition of success, you will see that there is no element of luck about it. A man may, and sometimes men do, fall into opportunities through mere chance or luck, but they have a queer way of falling out of those opportunities the first time opposition overtakes them.

HILL: Mr. Carnegie, in your definition of success, you used the word power. You said that success is achieved through the power with which to acquire whatever one wants.

CARNEGIE: Personal power is acquired through a combination of individual traits and habits, some of which will be explained in greater detail as we come to the remaining Principles of Achievement. Briefly, the ten qualities of personal power, which we call the 10-Point Rule of Personal Power are: 1) definiteness of purpose, 2) promptness of decision, 3) soundness of character or intentional honesty, 4) strict discipline over one's emotions, 5) obsessional desire to render useful service, 6) thorough knowledge of one's occupation, 7) tolerance on all subjects, 8) loyalty to one's personal associates and faith in a supreme being, 9) enduring thirst for knowledge, and 10) alertness of imagination.

You will observe that this 10-Point Rule embraces traits that anyone may develop. These traits lead to a form of personal power that can be used without violating the rights of others. That is the only form of personal power anyone can afford to wield.

CHAPTER 2

The Mastermind

HILL: Mr. Carnegie, we now come to the second of these principles, which you have named the Mastermind. Please define what you mean by the term.

CARNEGIE: The Mastermind is an alliance of two or more minds working together in the spirit of perfect harmony for the attainment of a definite purpose.

HILL: Do you mean to say, Mr. Carnegie, that the mere choice of a major purpose in life is not of itself enough to ensure success?

CARNEGIE: To achieve the object of one's major goal one must so relate himself to the members of his Mastermind alliance that he will procure the full benefit of their brains in a spirit of harmony. Before any alliance can constitute a Mastermind, everyone in the group must have his heart as well as his head in full sympathy with the object of the alliance, and he must be in perfect harmony with every other member of the alliance.

HILL: On previous occasions you have referred to nine major motives that unite people in the Mastermind alliance and life in general. Will you name them?

CARNEGIE: Here are the nine motives, some combination of which creates the moving spirit back of everything we do: 1) The emotion of love, the gateway to one's spiritual power. 2) The emotion of sex, which may serve as a powerful stimulant to action when transmuted. 3) Desire for financial gain. 4) Self-preservation. 5) Desire for freedom of body and mind. 6) Desire for self-expression leading to fame and recognition. 7) Desire for life after death.

The last two motives are negative but very powerful as stimulants to action. They are: 8) The emotion of anger often expressed as envy or jealousy. And, 9) The emotion of fear.

Here you have the nine major approaches to all minds. The leader of a successful Mastermind alliance must depend upon one or more of these basic motives to induce each member of his group to give the harmonious cooperation required for success.

HILL: Which emotions draw the greatest response?

CARNEGIE: The two motives to which men respond most generously in business alliances are the emotion of sex and the desire for financial gain. Most men want money more than any other thing, but they often want it mainly to please the woman of their choice. Here then, the motivating force is three-fold: love, sex, and financial gain. There is a type of man, however, who will work harder for recognition than he will for material and financial gains.

HILL: You say that all success of noteworthy proportions is the result of understanding and application of the Mastermind Principle. Are there not some exceptions to this rule, Mr. Carnegie? Couldn't a man become a great artist or a great preacher or a successful salesman without the use of the Mastermind Principle?

CARNEGIE: The answer is no. A man might become an artist or a preacher or a salesman without direct application of the Mastermind Principle, but he could not become great in these fields of endeavor without the aid of this principle. An all-wise providence has so arranged the mechanism of the mind that no single mind is complete. Richness of the mind in its fullest sense comes from the harmonious alliance of two or more minds working together toward the achievement of some definite purpose.

HILL: What is the plan for improving and maintaining romantic and household relationships, Mr. Carnegie?

CARNEGIE: The time would be well spent if married people set aside a regular hour for a confidential Mastermind meeting at least once every week during which they would come to an understanding concerning every vital factor of their relationship both in and outside of the home associations. Continuous contact between a man and his wife is an essential for harmony and cooperative effort.

HILL: Earlier you mentioned the key role of the sex emotion. Can you expand on this?

CARNEGIE: The emotion of sex is nature's own source of inspiration through which she gives both men and women the impelling desire to create, build, lead, and direct. Every great artist, every great musician, and every great dramatist gives expression to the emotion of sex transmuted into human endeavor. It is also true that men of vision, initiative, and enthusiasm who lead and excel in industry and business owe their superiority to transmuted sex emotion.

The well-informed man recognizes the possibilities available to him by combining the emotion of sex with whatever plan he adopts for the object of his Mastermind alliance with his wife. The same suggestion offers stupendous benefits to the married woman who is interested both in aiding her husband in his occupation and in holding his interest in herself. Let it be remembered, however, that the relationship of sex to be of enduring benefit as a medium of inspiration, must be kept on a high pedestal of romance.

HILL: Why do you stress the importance of romance?

CARNEGIE: Because wherever evidence of greatness in men is found, no matter in what age or calling, there one may also find evidence of this spirit of romance. The acorn yields an oak tree only in response to the stimulus of the sun's rays. The bird breaks the shell and takes to wing only in response to warmth outside itself. The seed of achievement that reposes in the brain of every man responds most quickly to the warmth of another's love and affection. Ignore the call of romance when it appeals to you from within and you hide your talents in the darkness of obscurity.

On the contrary, listen for the call of this messenger of infinite intelligence treated with civility and understanding when it arrives, and it will hand you the key to the temple of wisdom whose doors are locked within your heart and brain.

All that is great and good in man and woman comes to be there only through God's gift of love. Keep the fire of romance burning. Let it become a part, an important part, of the Mastermind ceremony, and your martial relationship will yield priceless returns in both material and spiritual measures.

HILL: From what you have said about the spirit of romance I get the impression that it is a great driving force that may be used in the pursuit of one's aim.

CARNEGIE: Precisely. The force that is born of a combination of love and sex is the elixir of life through which nature expresses all creative effort. Understand this truth, and you will know why a man's greatest use of the Mastermind Principle is that which grows out of his alliance with the mate of his choice.

The spirit of romance is born of the combination of the emotions of love and sex. Enthusiasm, driving force, keen interest, and vision are essential for success in any calling, and these states of mind can be produced at will by the person who converts the motives of sex and love, two of the strongest of the basic motives, into an obsessional interest in his occupation.

Chapter 3

Attractive Personality

Hill: Mr. Carnegie, we now come to the third of the 17 Principles of Individual Achievement, which you have named Attractive Personality. I understand that you have separated the factors behind personality into twenty-four distinct traits, all but one of which may be developed by anyone. Please describe these characteristics of personality with special emphasis on those that you consider of greatest importance.

Carnegie: I will not only describe the twenty-four traits of an Attractive Personality, but I will also give you a simple formula with which all but one of these traits may be developed and maintained.

We will begin with the outline of the twenty-four factors with a description of the most important of these, which is **positive mental attitude**. One may get a fair idea of the important part mental attitude plays in the affairs of an individual's life by considering the fact that it influences the tone of voice, the expression of the face, the posture of the body, and modifies every word that is spoken as well as determining the nature of every emotion one feels.

It does more than these. It modifies every thought one releases thereby extending its influences to all within its range through the principle of telepathy.

The second is **flexibility**. By this I mean the ability to adapt quickly to changing circumstances and emergencies without losing one's sense of balance. Without this ability, an attractive personality is hardly possible, as the ever-changing conditions of life and of human relationships require individual adaptability.

The third is **sincerity of purpose**. This is one trait of character for which there is no substitute. I say it is a trait of character because it is something that reaches deeper into a human being than any mere quality of personality. Sincerity of purpose, or the lack of it, writes itself so indelibly into the words and deeds of men that even the novice at character analysis can recognize its presence or absence.

The fourth factor is **promptness of decision**. Those who dillydally around trying to make up their minds are neither popular nor successful. This is a fast-moving world, and those who do not move quickly cannot keep up. Successful men reach decisions definitely and quickly, and they become annoyed and inconvenienced by others who do not act promptly.

I call your attention also to the close relationship between promptness of decision and definiteness of purpose. The man with the vision to recognize opportunity and the promptness of decision to embrace it will get ahead. This is the way of the world. It always makes a place for the man who knows exactly what he wants and is determined to get it.

Courtesy is the fifth factor. It is an essential part of an attractive personality. And it is absolutely free. All it costs is the time required to express it in one's daily contact with others. Perhaps its very cheapness accounts for its scarcity, as it is so rare that when one comes upon it one is quick to take note of the person expressing it. Courtesy simply means respecting other people's feelings under all circumstances, going out of one's way to help any less fortunate person whenever possible, and controlling selfishness in all its forms. Courtesy is a medium with which one may project his influence to sources of opportunity he could not reach without it.

Number six is **tone of voice**. The spoken word is, by great odds, the medium through which one expresses his personality most often, therefore, the tone of one's voice should be so thoroughly under control that it can be colored and modified so as to make it carry a meaning quite in addition to the mere words expressed, for it does carry a separate meaning, whether one is conscious of this or not. The idea, therefore, is to so cultivate the voice that it can be used to convey the particular meaning desired.

Factor seven is the **habit of smiling**. Now, don't make the mistake of feeling that this simple habit of smiling is not important, and don't forget that it is a habit that is directly associated with mental attitude. If you aren't sure about this, just try smiling when you are angry. I suggest that one should stand before a mirror when practicing voice control because there are certain expressions of speech that cannot be dramatized properly unless they are accompanied by a smile.

The eighth factor is **facial expression**. You can tell a great deal of what is going on in one's mind by the expression on his face. Master salesmen can tell by careful observation of a prospective buyer's facial expression much about what his real thoughts are. If they cannot do this, they are not master salesmen. Moreover, the cleverest salesman also learns to judge what is going on in the other fellow's mind by the tone of his voice. Thus, the smile, the tone of voice, the expression of the face constitute an open window through which all who will may see and feel what takes place in the minds of people. This naturally suggests to the smart person the use of caution in connection with this open window. The smart person will know when to keep the window closed. He also will know when to open it.

We are up to number nine, which is **tactfulness**. There is always a right and a wrong time for everything. Tactfulness consists of the habit of doing and saying the right thing at the right time, and I'm going to enumerate for you a list of the more common ways in which people show their lack of tactfulness: 1) Carelessness in tone, often speaking in gruff, antagonistic tones. 2) Speaking out of turn when silence would be more appropriate. 3) Interrupting others. 4) Constantly referring to yourself. 5) Asking impertinent questions. 6) Injecting intimately personal subjects into conversation where such action is embarrassing to others. 7) Going where one has not been invited. 8) Boastfulness. 9) Flouting the rules of society in matters of personal adornment. 10) Making personal calls at inconvenient hours. 11) Holding people on the telephone with needless conversation. 12) Writing people whom one has no reasonable excuse for addressing. 13) Volunteering opinions when not asked. 14) Openly questioning the soundness of others' opinions. 15) Declining requests in an arrogant manner. 16) Disparaging people in front of their friends. 17) Rebuking those who disagree with you. 18) Speaking of people's physical afflictions in their presence. 19) Correcting subordinates and associates in the presence of others. 20) Complaining when requests for favors are refused. 21) Presuming upon friendship in asking favors. 22) Using profane or offensive language. 23) Expressing dislikes too freely. 24) Speaking of ills and misfortunes. 25) Criticizing some other person's religion. 26) Overfamiliarity on all occasions.

Tenth place goes to **tolerance**. Let us define tolerance simply as open-mindedness. The tolerant person is one who holds his mind open for new facts, knowledge, and viewpoints on all subjects. Observe, too, how closely related are tolerance and tactfulness.

The eleventh trait of Attractive Personality is **frankness of manner and speech**. Everyone mistrusts the man who resorts to subterfuge instead of dealing frankly with his daily associates. I have known men who were so slippery that you could not pin them down to a direct, clear-cut statement on any subject. I have never yet seen a man of this type who could be depended upon. This sort of man doesn't come right out and lie, but he does what amounts to exactly the same thing by deliberately withholding important facts. Men of sound character always have the courage to speak and deal directly with people, and they follow this habit even though it may, at times, be to their personal disadvantage. Men who resort to subterfuge to deceive others seldom have very much confidence in themselves.

Number twelve is **a keen sense of humor**. A well-developed sense of humor aids a man in becoming flexible and adjustable to the varying circumstances of life. It keeps a man from taking himself and life too seriously, a tendency toward which altogether too many people are inclined. A sense of humor even serves to give one a better physical appearance, as it helps to keep the lines of the face softened. It also leads to the habit of smiling, which is one of the important traits of Attractive Personality, and there is a definite relationship between a sense of humor and mental attitude. A keen sense of humor encourages a positive mental attitude.

Now we come to the most profound and far-reaching of all the elements comprising an Attractive Personality: **Faith in Infinite Intelligence**. Faith is woven into every principle of the Philosophy of Achievement since the intangible power of faith is the essence of every great achievement, no matter what may be its nature or purpose. In short, the power that operates the exquisitely finely tuned machine called the brain is a form of energy which comes from the outside, and faith is the master gate through which an individual may give his brain full and free access to the great universal power which operates it.

The hand that opens the gate and permits the free entry of the power that operates the brain is desire or motive. No one has ever discovered any other method of opening the gate. There are various degrees to which it can be opened, all depending upon motive and desire. Only those desires which take on the proportion of an obsession, burning desires, serve to open wide the valve.

A burning desire in the sense that I am using this term is one that is accompanied by a deep, emotional feeling. Mere head desires growing out of pure reason do not open the gate to the brain as widely as heart desires that are mixed with emotion. I wish to make this point very clear and to emphasize it in every way possible *for it is the very warp and woof of the subject of faith.*

The next trait is a **keen sense of justice**. It seems trite to remind people that an individual cannot hope to become popular and attractive unless he deals justly with others. Justice, as I use the term means intentional honesty. Many people are honest for the sake of expediency, but their brand of honesty is so flexible that they can stretch it to fit any circumstance. We are talking about deliberate honesty that is so rigidly adhered to that the individual is motivated by it under circumstances that may not be to his immediate benefit, the same as to those that promise the greatest possible reward. In addition to its many benefits, this establishes a basis of confidence, without which no one can have an attractive personality. It builds a fundamentally sincere and sound character which of itself is one of the greatest of all attracting forces. It not only attracts people, but it offers opportunities for personal gain in one's occupation. It gives one a feeling of self-reliance and self-respect.

Number fifteen is **appropriateness of words**. Among cultured people, there is perhaps no greater source of annoyance than the careless use of words. Colloquialisms and slang may be passable at times, but the less these are used, the better. Proper use of language is an indelible mark of culture and persuasiveness.

The sixteenth trait of an attractive personality is **emotional control**. Most of us are directed less by reason than by emotion. We do things, or we refrain from doing them because of *how we feel*. Emotion, therefore, may be defined with one word: feeling. This is a mighty important word since it defines the motivating force that controls most of our actions throughout life. We certainly owe it to ourselves to learn as much as possible about the force that lifts us to great achievement or hurls us downward to defeat.

The seventeenth trait may be called **alertness of interest in persons, places, and things**. Without the ability to fix one's interest at will on any subject or person and hold it there for whatever time the occasion requires, no one will have an attractive personality. You can pay another person no greater compliment, generally speaking, than that of concentrating your attention upon him when he desires your attention.

The eighteenth trait of an attractive personality is **effective speech.** The person who cannot stand on his feet and speak with force and conviction on any subject within his range of knowledge is under a great handicap. The same applies to the man who cannot express himself forcefully in ordinary conversation and in small-group gatherings such as business conferences. The ability to dramatize words and express them forcefully at all times, under all conditions, is among the greatest of human achievements. In fact, some people place this power at the head of the list of all personal achievements.

The ability to dramatize speech comes through habit. Therefore, one should begin this habit by speaking forcefully in ordinary conversation. There is where great speakers learn the art of effective speech. They practice on every person with whom they converse. They never utter a word without placing back of it the necessary feeling to make it penetrate the mind of the listener. This simple procedure will make an effective speaker of anyone who follows it as a matter of daily habit.

The nineteenth trait of a pleasing personality is **versatility**. It is hardly necessary to mention the obvious fact that people who lack a general understanding of their world, including at least a surface knowledge of human nature, are seldom interesting or attractive. A general interest in things and people is one of the essentials of flexibility of personality.

The twentieth trait is a **genuine fondness for people**. People recognize individuals who like people, and they resent those who have a natural distain. The Law of Retribution always operates so that people are judged and dealt with, not alone by their deeds, but by their dominating mental attitudes. It is inevitable, therefore, that the person who dislikes people will be disliked.

The twenty-first trait is **humility of the heart.** Arrogance, greed, vanity, and egotism are never found in the man who has a pleasing personality.

Number twenty-two is **good showmanship**. Showmanship is the ability to combine facial expression, tone of voice, personal adornment, choice of words, control of the emotions, courtesy, effective speech, versatility, mental attitude, sense of humor, emphasis, and tactfulness in such a manner as to dramatize any circumstance or occasion so as to attract favorable attention.

The twenty-third trait is **clean sportsmanship**. The man who can win without boasting and lose without squealing generally has the admiration of other people.

The twenty-fourth and final trait is **personal magnetism**. Let us be frank at the outset and say that personal magnetism is a polite way of describing sex energy, for that is precisely what it means. Now, we need not evade the admission that sex energy is something with which an individual is born, and it therefore cannot be developed by personal effort. Sex energy is nature's own device with which she creates and perpetuates every living thing from God's smallest creature to his greatest handiwork, man. I see no reason, therefore, for subterfuge in connection with the analysis of sex emotion as one of the most important traits of personality, but I do see a reason for making it plain that this universal power adds attractive qualities to the personality only when it is controlled and used properly.

I am referring to transmutation, which means diverting sex emotion from physical expression into whatever constructive purpose one wishes to carry out. It is a well-known fact that when a man who is highly sexed organizes this irresistible, creative force and places it at the back of his occupational endeavors, he has but little difficulty in persuading people to cooperate with him.

The emotion of sex must be considered as one of the most important factors of an attractive personality. Therefore, I have given here a clue from which anyone smart enough to recognize it may add greatly to his ability to influence people through his personality.

CHAPTER 4

Applied Faith

HILL: Mr. Carnegie, how may one develop faith?

CARNEGIE: Clearing the mind of its enemies may develop faith. Clear the mind of negative thoughts, fears, and self-imposed limitations, and faith fills the place without effort. There is no great mystery about the state of mind known as faith. Give it a place to dwell, and it will move in without ceremony or invitation.

HILL: From what you have said, Mr. Carnegie, the best way to start developing faith is by choosing an objective and beginning at once to attain it through whatever media available.

CARNEGIE: Exactly. The development of faith is largely a matter of understanding the astounding power of the mind. The only real mystery about faith is man's failure to make use of it. I speak from personal experience when I say that faith is a state of mind that can be acquired and used as effectively and easily as any other state of mind. It is all a matter of understanding and application. Truly, faith without works is dead.

My early days of youth were cursed by poverty and limitation of opportunity, a fact with which all who know me are acquainted. I am no longer cursed by poverty because I took possession of my mind, and that mind has yielded to me every material thing I want and much more than I need. Faith is no patented right of mind. It is a universal power as available to the humblest person as it is to the greatest.

CHAPTER 5

Going The Extra Mile

HILL: Mr. Carnegie, I have heard some men say that success is often the result of luck. Do you attribute any portion of your success to luck or favorable breaks?

CARNEGIE: Your question gives me a starting point for describing the fifth of the 17 Principles of Achievement, which is called the Habit of Going the Extra Mile. This means rendering more service and better service than one is paid for.

First, I will answer your question by saying yes, indeed, there is a wheel of life that controls human destinies, and I am happy to be able to tell you that this wheel can be definitely *influenced* to operate in one's favor. If this were not true, there would be no object in organizing the rules of personal achievement.

First of all, to control the wheel of fortune, one must understand and apply the 17 Principles of Achievement. Now, the habit of doing more than one is paid for is one that an individual may practice without asking the permission of others. Therefore, it is under one's own control. Many other beneficial habits can be practiced only through the consent and cooperation of other people.

Until a man begins to render more service than that for which he is paid, he is not entitled to more pay than he receives for that service since, obviously, he is already receiving full pay for what he does.

I think I can make the point clear by calling attention to the simple illustration of the farmer. Before he collects pay for his services, he carefully and intelligently prepares the soil, plows and harrows it, fertilizes it if need be, then plants it with seed. Up to this point, he has gained nothing whatsoever for his labor, but understanding the Law of Growth as he does, he rests after his labor while nature germinates the seed and yields him a crop.

Here, the element of time enters into the farmer's labor. In due time, nature gives him back the seed he planted in the ground together with an abundant overplus to compensate him for his labor and his knowledge. If he sows a bushel of wheat in properly prepared soil, he gets back the bushel of seed together with, perhaps, as many as ten additional bushels as his compensation.

Here, the Law of Increasing Returns has stepped in and compensated the farmer for his effort and his intelligence. If there were no such law, man could not exist on this earth since obviously there would be no object in planting a bushel of wheat in the ground if nature yielded back only a bushel of grain.

It is this over-plus which nature yields through the Law of Increasing Returns that makes it possible for man to produce from the ground, but little imagination is needed to see that the man who renders more service and better service than that for which he is paid thereby places himself in a position to benefit by this same law.

Often, I have heard working men say, "I'm not paid to do that," or, "This is not my responsibility." You've heard statements like that. Everyone has. Well, when you hear a man talking like this, you may mark him down as one who will never get more than a bare living from his work. Moreover, that sort of mental attitude makes one disliked by his associates, and it therefore discourages favorable opportunities for self-promotion.

Successful men are not looking for short hours and easy jobs, for if they are truly successful, they know that no such circumstance exists. Successful men are always looking for ways to lengthen instead of shorten the working days.

Emerson said, "Do the thing, and you shall have the power." He never expressed a more truthful thought. It applies to every calling and to every human relationship. Men who gain and hold power do so by making themselves useful to others.

CHAPTER 6

Organized Individual Endeavor

HILL: You have stated, Mr. Carnegie, that Organized Individual Endeavor is the sixth of the 17 Principles of Individual Achievement. Will you analyze this principle in its relationship to personal achievement?

CARNEGIE: Personal initiative may be likened to the steam in the boiler in this respect. It is the power through which one's plans, aims, and purposes are put into action. It is the antithesis of one of the worst of all human traits, procrastination. Successful men are known always as men of action. There can be no action without the exercise of one's initiative. There are two forms of action: 1) that in which one indulges from force of necessity; and 2) that which one exercises out of choice of his own free will. Leadership grows from the latter. It comes as the result of action in which one engages in response to his own motives and desires.

HILL: When, and under what circumstances, should one begin to exercise personal initiative?

CARNEGIE: The time to begin using personal initiative is immediately following one's definite decision as to what one wishes to accomplish. The time to begin is right then. If the plan chosen turns out to be weak, it can be changed for a better one, but any sort of plan is better than procrastination. The universal evil of the world is procrastination, the terrible habit people have of waiting for the time to begin something to be just right. It causes more failures than all the weak plans of the world.

HILL: But, shouldn't one consult others and get their opinions before beginning important plans?

CARNEGIE: Opinions are like the sands of the desert, and most of them are about as slippery. Everyone has an opinion about practically everything, but most of them are unworthy of trust. The man who hesitates because he wants the opinion of others before he begins to exercise his personal initiative usually winds up by doing nothing.

Of course, there are exceptions to this rule. There are times when the counsel and advice of others are absolutely essential for success, but if you refer to idle opinions of bystanders, let them alone. Avoid them as you would an epidemic of disease for that is exactly what idle opinions are, a disease. Everyone has a flock of them, and most people hand them out freely without being asked. When you need information for your endeavor, seek expertise—never opinion.

CHAPTER 7

Creative Vision

HILL: Mr. Carnegie, you have said that Creative Vision is the seventh Principle of Individual Achievement. Will you analyze this principle and describe how to use it?

CARNEGIE: First of all, let us have a clear understanding of the meaning of the term Creative Vision as we are using it by explaining that this is but another name for imagination. There are two types of imagination. One is known as *synthetic imagination* and the other as *creative imagination.*

   Synthetic imagination consists of the act of combining recognized ideas, concepts, plans, facts, and principles in new arrangements. The old axiom that there is nothing new under the sun grew out of the fact that the majority of things that seemed to be new are nothing but a rearrangement of that which is old. Practically all the patents recorded in the patent office are nothing more than old ideas that have been arranged in a new order or given a new use.

Creative imagination has its source, as far as science has been able to determine, in the subconscious mind wherein exists through some power unknown to science, the ability to perceive and interpret basically new ideas. It is believed by some that the faculty of a creative imagination truly is the workshop of the soul through which man may contact and be guided by infinite intelligence. Of this, however, there is no conclusive evidence save only that which is circumstantial.

Let us, therefore, be content to accept the reality of creative imagination and make the best possible use of it without endeavoring to define its source. Of one fact we can be sure, and that is the undeniable reality of the existence of a faculty of the mind through which some men perceive and interpret new ideas never before known to man.

HILL: Which of the two types of imagination is used more often in business?

CARNEGIE: Synthetic imagination is more commonly used. Creative imagination, as the name implies, is used only by those who, generally speaking, have attained to some form of leadership or unusual skill. Inventors and artists rely on creative imagination. To tap into this power you must intensify your desires until they become obsessional. A deep, burning desire is picked up by the subconscious and acted upon much more definitely and quickly than an ordinary desire. A mere wish appears to make no impression on the subconscious. Many people become confused as to the difference between a wish and a burning desire that has been stimulated into obsessional proportions by the repetition of thought in connection with the desire.

HILL: Then, anyone may make use of creative imagination by the simple process of charging his subconscious mind with definite desires?

CARNEGIE: Yes, there is nothing to hinder anyone from using this principle, but you must remember that practical results are obtained only by those who have gained discipline over their thought habits through the process of concentration of interest in desire. Fleeting thoughts, which come and go intermittently and mere wishes, which are about the extent of the average person's thinking, make no impression whatsoever on the subconscious mind.

HILL: Why is it that so few people appear to have a well-developed imagination?

CARNEGIE: The faculty of imagination, like all other faculties of the mind, can be developed through use. The reason so many people seem not to have a keen imagination is obvious. Most people allow the faculty of imagination to atrophy through neglect. But in those with a strong enough desire it builds.

Chapter 8

Self-Discipline

Hill: Mr. Carnegie, you have designated Self-Discipline as the eighth Principle of Individual Achievement. Please describe the part that self-discipline plays in personal achievement and how to cultivate it.

Carnegie: Self-discipline begins with the mastery of one's thoughts. Without control over thoughts, there can be no control over deeds. Let us say, therefore, that self-discipline inspires one to think first and to act afterward. The usual procedure is just the reverse. Most people act first and think afterward, if and when they think at all. Thinking is power.

Hill: I judge from what you have said previously that personal power is something that must be used with discretion, or it may turn out to be a curse instead of a blessing.

CARNEGIE: I've always made it a part of my business philosophy to caution my associates against the dangers of indiscreet use of personal power and especially those who, through promotions, have but recently come into the possession of increased power. Newly acquired power is something like newly acquired riches. It needs watching closely lest a man become the victim of his own power.

Here is where self-discipline gives a good account of itself. If a man has his own mind under complete control, he makes it serve him in a manner that does not antagonize other people.

HILL: I deduce that self-discipline is largely a matter of the adoption of constructive habits.

CARNEGIE: That is precisely the idea. That which a man is, that which he accomplishes, both his failures and his successes are the results of his habits. Fortunately, habits are self-formed. They are under the control of the individual. The most important of these are the habits of thought. A man finally comes to resemble in his deeds the nature of his thought habits. When he gains control over his thought habits, he has gone a long way toward the attainment of self-discipline.

Definite motives are the beginning of thought habits. It is not difficult for a man to keep his mind on the thing that serves as his greatest motive, especially if the motive becomes obsessional. Self-discipline without definiteness of motive is impossible. Moreover, it would be without value.

HILL: In terms of discipline, should a man attempt to control his life with his reasoning faculty and leave the emotions out of his decisions and plans?

CARNEGIE: That would be very unwise, even if it were possible. Emotions provide the driving power, the action force that enables a man to put his head decisions into operation. The aim is control and discipline of the emotions, not elimination. The emotions of man are something like a river in that their power can be damned up and released in whatever proportions and whatever directions one desires, but they cannot be eliminated. Through self-discipline, a man can organize all his emotions and release them in a highly concentrated form as a means of attaining the object of his plans and purpose.

The two most powerful emotions are love and sex. These emotions are inborn, the handiwork of nature, the instruments through which the Creator provided for both the perpetuation of the human race and for social integration by which civilization evolves from a lower to a higher order of human relationship. One would hardly wish to destroy so great a gift as the emotions, even if this were possible for the reason that they represent man's greatest power.

If you destroy hope and faith, what would you have left that would be of use to man? If you remove enthusiasm, loyalty, and the desire for achievement, you would still have left the faculty of reason, the head power, but what good would it be? There would be nothing left for the head to direct.

Now, let me call your attention to an astounding truth. The emotions of hope, faith, enthusiasm, loyalty, and desire are nothing but specialized applications of the inborn emotions of love and sex diverted or transmuted into different purposes. As a matter of fact, every human emotion outside of love and sex has its roots in these two natural inborn traits of man. If these two natural emotions were destroyed in a man, he would become as docile as a domesticated animal.

HILL: Self-discipline, then, is the tool with which a man may harness and direct his inborn emotions in whatever direction he chooses?

CARNEGIE: That is correct. Now, I wish to call your attention to another astounding truth. Creative Vision is the result of self-discipline through which the emotions of love and sex are transmuted into some specialized plan or purpose. There has never yet been born a great leader in any form of human endeavor who did not attain his leadership by mastery and direction of these two great inborn emotions.

The great artists, musicians, writers, speakers, lawyers, doctors, architects, inventors, scientists, industrialists, salesmen, and the outstanding men and women in all walks of life attain their leadership by harnessing and directing their natural emotions of love and sex as a driving force behind their endeavors. In most instances, the diversion of these emotions into specialized endeavor is done unconsciously as the result of a burning desire for achievement. In some instances, the transmutation is deliberate.

HILL: Then, it is no disgrace for one to be born with great capacity for the emotions of love and sex.

CARNEGIE: No. The disgrace comes from the abuse of these natural gifts. The abuse is the result of ignorance, the lack of training as to the nature and potentialities of these great emotions.

HILL: I get the impression that the most important application of self-discipline is that through which one takes possession of his sex emotion and transforms it into whatever form of endeavor he desires. Is that true?

CARNEGIE: Yes, and I may add that when a man once acquires discipline over his sex emotion, he will find it easy to discipline himself in all other directions, and the reason for this is that the emotion of sex reflects itself either consciously or unconsciously in practically everything a man does. Failure to gain control over the emotions of love and sex generally means failure to gain control over other traits.

CHAPTER 9

Organized Thinking

HILL: You have explained that the ninth Principle of Individual Achievement is Organized Thought. You have also stated that no one may be sure of success without the ability to organize his thinking habits. I have a general idea what it means, but I would like to have a detailed statement of its meaning.

CARNEGIE: Before discussing the organization of thought, let us examine thought itself. What is thought? With what do we think? Is thought subject to individual control? Thought is a form of energy that is distributed through the brain, but it has one peculiar quality unknown in connection with all other forms of energy.

It has intelligence. Thought can be controlled and directed toward the attainment of anything man may desire. In fact, thought is the only thing over which any person has complete, unchallenged control. The system of control is so complete that no one may penetrate the mind of another without his consent although this system of protection often is so loosely guarded that one's mind may be entered at will by any person skilled in the art of thought interpretation.

Many people not only leave their minds wide open for others to enter and interpret their thoughts, but they voluntarily disclose the nature of their thoughts by unguarded expressions of speech and their personal conduct, their facial expression, and the like.

HILL: Is it safe for one to leave his mind open to free entry by others?

CARNEGIE: Just about as safe as leaving the door to one's house unlocked with all of one's valuables left inside the house, except that the loss of purely material things is as nothing compared with the loss one may suffer by leaving his mind open to entry by any stray who may wish to go in and take possession.

The habit of leaving one's mind open and unguarded not only permits other people to enter and become familiar with one's most private thoughts, but this habit permits all sorts of errant thoughts released from the minds of others to enter one's mind.

HILL: You believe, then, that thoughts do pass from one mind to another through the principle of telepathy?

CARNEGIE: That fact has apparently been established by men of science, but I have evidence of its existence from my own personal experience. Yes, one's mind is being constantly bombarded with the impulses of thought released from the minds of others, especially those with whom we come into close contact daily. That is one of the major reasons why I have emphasized the importance of harmony. The chemistry of the brain is such that the mind power of a group of men can be organized so it functions as one unit of power only when there is perfect rapport between the minds of the individuals.

HILL: One of the important steps in Organized Thought seems to be that of the Mastermind alliance through which men pool their mind power, their experience, education, and knowledge and move in response to a common motive. Is this the right idea, Mr. Carnegie?

CARNEGIE: You have stated the matter perfectly. You might have said that the Mastermind alliance is the most important step one may take in connection with Organized Thought, for that is true, but Organized Thought begins with the organization of the individual's thinking habits. To become an effective member of a Mastermind alliance, an individual must first form definite, controlled habits of thought. A group of men working together under the Mastermind principle, each of whom has so disciplined himself that he controls his thought habits, represents Organized Thought of the highest order.

As a matter of fact, there can never be full assurance of harmony in a Mastermind group unless each member of the group is so self-disciplined that he can control his own thoughts.

HILL: Do I understand you to say that an individual may actually discipline himself so that he controls the nature of his thoughts?

CARNEGIE: That is true, but remember that one gains control over his thoughts by forming definite thought habits. You know, of course, that when habits are once formed, they function automatically without any voluntary effort on the individual's part.

HILL: But, isn't it very difficult for one to force his mind to function through definite habits? How may one go about this sort of self-discipline?

CARNEGIE: No. There is nothing difficult about the formation of habits. As a matter of fact, the mind is constantly forming thought habits without the conscious knowledge of the individual responding, as the mind does, to every influence that reaches it from one's daily environment.

Through self-discipline, one may switch the action of his mind from the response to the casual influences around him to subjects of his own choice. This is accomplished by setting up in the mind a definite motive based on a definite purpose and intensifying that purpose until it becomes an obsession.

HILL: Then, Organized Thought begins with Definiteness of Purpose?

CARNEGIE: Everything man achieves begins with Definiteness of Purpose. Name a single instance, if you can, where a man has achieved any form of success without a definite motive based on a definite purpose carried out through a definite plan, but you must remember that there is one more factor that must be considered in connection with Definiteness of Purpose. The purpose must be expressed in terms of intense action.

Here is where the power of the emotions gives an account of itself. The emotional feeling of desire for the attainment of a definite purpose is the power that gives life and action to that purpose and influences one to move on his own initiative.

To ensure satisfactory results, one's definite purpose should be given obsessional proportions. It should be backed by a burning desire for its attainment. Desires of this sort take full possession of one's mind and keep it so fully occupied that it has no inclination or opportunity to entertain stray thoughts released by the minds of others.

HILL: I believe I see what you mean. For example, a young man who is in love has no difficulty in keeping his mind on the object of his love, and not infrequently, his mind works out ways and means of inducing response to his affections from the woman of his choice. In this sort of circumstance, one has no difficulty in forming controlled thought habits.

CARNEGIE: A good illustration. Now, switch it over to some other sort of purpose such, for example, as the development of a business or a profession or the attainment of a definite position or the accumulation of money, and you will have an idea of how these ends are attained, through obsessional desire for their attainment.

CHAPTER 10

Learning from Defeat

HILL: Mr. Carnegie, you have stated that defeat can be converted into a priceless asset if one takes the right attitude toward it. Will you explain that right attitude?

CARNEGIE: The right attitude toward defeat is that which refuses to accept it as anything more than temporary, and this is an attitude that one can best maintain by so developing his willpower that he looks upon defeat as a challenge to test his mettle. That challenge should be accepted as a signal that has been deliberately hoisted to inform him that his plans need mending.

Defeat should be looked upon in precisely the same manner that one accepts the unpleasant experience of physical pain, for it is obvious that physical pain is nature's way of informing one that something needs attention and correction. Pain, therefore, may be a blessing and not a curse.

The same is true of the mental anguish one experiences when overtaken by defeat. While the feeling is unpleasant, it may be nevertheless beneficial because it serves as a signal by which one may be stopped from going in the wrong direction.

HILL: I see your logic, but defeat sometimes is so definite and severe that it has the effect of destroying one's initiative and self-reliance. What is to be done in such a circumstance?

CARNEGIE: Here is where the Principle of Self-Discipline comes to one's rescue. The well-disciplined person allows nothing to destroy his belief in himself and permits nothing to stop him from rearranging his plans and moving ahead when he is defeated. You see, he changes his plans if they need change but not his purpose. If one has mastered the Principle of Organized Thought, one knows that the power of will is equal to all the circumstances of life. He allows nothing to destroy his will to win.

HILL: You mean, I assume, that defeat should be accepted as a sort of mental tonic that can be made to serve as a means of stimulating one's willpower.

CARNEGIE: You've stated it correctly. As I told you previously, *every negative emotion can be transmuted into a constructive power and used for the attainment of desirable ends.* Self-discipline enables one to change unpleasant emotions into a driving power, and every time this is done, it helps to develop one's power of will.

You must remember also that the subconscious mind accepts and acts upon one's mental attitude. If defeat is accepted as permanent instead of being regarded as a mere stimulant to greater action, the subconscious mind acts accordingly and makes it permanent. You see, therefore, how important it is that one form the habit of searching for the good there is to be found in every form of defeat. This procedure becomes the finest sort of training of the willpower and serves, at the same time, to bring the subconscious mind into action in one's behalf.

CHAPTER 11

Inspiration

HILL: Mr. Carnegie, your eleventh Principle of Individual Achievement is Inspiration. You also call this Applied Enthusiasm. How may one develop this?

CARNEGIE: Inspiration is the result of desire expressed in terms of action and based upon motive. Inspiration is a form of animation that creates enthusiasm. No normal person ever goes into a heat of enthusiasm without a motive. It is obvious, therefore, that the beginning of all enthusiasm is desire based on motive. Enthusiasm, which is an expression of one or more of the emotions, stimulates the vibration of thought and makes it more intense, thus starting the faculty of the imagination to work in connection with the motive which inspired the enthusiasm. Enthusiasm gives tone quality to one's voice and makes it pleasing and impressive. A salesman or public speaker would be ineffective without the ability to turn on his enthusiasm at will. The same is true of one who engages in ordinary conversation. Even the most prosaic subjects can be made interesting if they are expressed with enthusiasm. Without it, the most interesting subjects can become tiresome.

Enthusiasm inspires initiative both in thought and in physical action. It is very difficult for one to do well at that for which he has no feeling of enthusiasm. Enthusiasm dispels physical fatigue and overcomes laziness. It has been said that there are no lazy men. What appears to be a lazy man is one who is moved by no motive over which he becomes enthusiastic.

Enthusiasm stimulates the entire nervous system and causes it to perform its duties more efficiently including, in particular, the function of digestion of food. For this reason, the meal hour should be the pleasantest hour of the day, and it should never become the occasion for settling personal or family differences of opinion, nor should it become the time for the correction of the faults of the children.

Enthusiasm stimulates the subconscious section of the brain and puts it to work in connection with the motive, which inspires enthusiasm. In fact, there is no known method of stimulating the subconscious mind voluntarily except that of inspired feeling.

Here, let us emphasize the fact that the subconscious mind acts upon all feeling, whether it is negative or positive. It will act on the emotion of fear as quickly as it will act on the emotion of love, or it will go to work on the worry over poverty as quickly as it will act on the feeling of opulence. It is important, therefore, to recognize that enthusiasm is the positive expression of feeling.

HILL: Is it not possible for one to display too much enthusiasm for his own good?

CARNEGIE: Yes. Uncontrolled enthusiasm often is as detrimental as no enthusiasm. For example, the man who is so enthusiastic over himself and his own ideas that he monopolizes the conversation when conversing with others is sure to be unpopular.

Then there is the man who becomes too enthusiastic over the roulette wheel or the horses and the man who becomes more enthusiastic over ways and means of getting something for nothing than he does over rendering useful service. This sort of uncontrolled enthusiasm may be very detrimental.

But enthusiasm directed toward constructive ends, and properly controlled by Organized Thinking, can heighten the vibrations of thought in such a way as to elevate a man into the category known as genius.

CHAPTER 12

Controlled Attention

HILL: Mr. Carnegie, you have named the twelfth principle of the Philosophy of Individual Achievement, Controlled Attention. Please describe how this principle can be applied in the practical affairs of life.

CARNEGIE: Controlled Attention is the act of combining all the faculties of the mind and concentrating them upon the attainment of a definite purpose. The time involved in the act of concentration of thought on a given subject depends upon the nature of the subject and upon that which one expects in connection with it.

Take my own case, for example. The dominating forces of my mind are, and have been for many years, concentrated upon the making and marketing of steel. I have others allied with me who likewise concentrate their dominating thoughts upon the same objective.

Thus, we have the benefit of Controlled Attention in collective form consisting as it does of the individual mind power of a great number of people, all working toward the same end, in a spirit of harmony.

It is important to note that splitting one's attention has the effect of dividing one's powers. The best plan for anyone to follow is to devote all his energies to some specific field. This concentration enables one to specialize in that field. Specialization through concentration of effort gives one greater power. It saves lost motion in both thought and physical action. It harmonizes with the Principle of Definiteness of Purpose, the starting point of all achievement.

CHAPTER 13

The Golden Rule Applied

CARNEGIE: We now come to the 13th Principle of Individual Achievement, The Golden Rule Applied, the principle which nearly everyone professes to believe, but few people practice, due I suspect, to the fact that so few people understand the deep underlying psychology of this principle.

The real benefits of the Golden Rule Applied do not come from those in whose favor it is applied, but they accrue to the one applying the rule in the form of a strengthened conscience, peace of mind, and the other attributes of sound character, the factors which attract the more desirable things of life, including enduring friendships and fortune.

To get the most from the Golden Rule, it must be combined with the Principle of Going the Extra Mile, wherein consists the applied portion of the Golden Rule. The Golden Rule supplies the right mental attitude while Going the Extra Mile supplies the action feature of this great rule. A combination of the two gives one the power of attraction which induces friendly cooperation from others as well as opportunities for personal accumulation.

Passive belief in this rule will accomplish nothing. It is the application of the rule that brings benefits, and they are so numerous and varied that they touch life through almost every human relationship. These are some of the more important benefits.

A, the Golden Rule Applied opens the mind for the guidance of Infinite Intelligence through faith.

B, develops self-reliance through a better relationship with one's conscience.

C, builds sound character sufficient to sustain one in times of emergency; develops a more attractive personality.

D, attracts the friendly cooperation of others in all human relationships.

E, discourages unfriendly opposition from others.

F, gives one peace of mind and freedom from self-established limitations.

G, gives one immunity against the more damaging forms of fear since the man with a clear conscience seldom fears anything or anyone.

H, enables one to go to prayer with clean hands and a clear heart.

I, attracts favorable opportunities for self-promotion in one's occupation, business, or profession.

J, eliminates the desire for something for nothing.

K, makes the rendering of useful service a joy that can be had in no other way.

L, provides one with an influential reputation for honesty and fair dealing, which is the basis of all confidence.

M, serves as a discouragement to the slanderer and a reprimand to the thief.

N, makes one a power for good, by example, whenever he comes into contact with others.

O, discourages all the baser instincts of greed and envy and revenge, and gives wings to the higher instincts of love and fellowship.

P, brings one within easy communicating distance of the Creator through the medium of an undisturbed mind.

Q, enables one to recognize the joys of accepting the truth that every man is, and by right should be, his brother's keeper.

R, establishes a deeper personal spirituality.

These are no mere opinions of mine. They are self-evident truths, the soundness of which is known to every person who lives by the Golden Rule as a matter of daily habit.

CHAPTER 14

Cooperation

HILL: In terms of the fourteenth Principle of the Philosophy of Achievement, do you mean that friendly cooperation is necessary for success?

CARNEGIE: Personal power is acquired through friendly coordination of effort and in no other way. In this country, we have an economic system based upon this sort of cooperation. That is why ours is the richest and most powerful nation in the world. We have found a practical way of coordinating the efforts of groups of individuals in all walks of life, and this coordination has given us great power.

If you are a close observer, you will have noticed that the individuals who have attained the highest degree of cooperation in their relationships with others are those who have achieved the greatest success in their chosen callings.

HILL: You believe then that government regulation of industry is for the common good of all. Why?

CARNEGIE: Because regulation within the bounds of reason discourages the greedy and the selfish individuals from seeking monopolies and protects the public against unfair practices in business.

Just as there must be unbiased umpires who see that the rules of the game are observed for the benefit of all the players, there must also be an unbiased governmental umpire who will see that the sound rules of industry are carried out for the benefit of all.

Every well-managed business has executives who see to it that all individuals work together in a spirit of teamwork. These executives serve as the umpires who coordinate all factors essential for the successful operation of the business. Their sense of fairness and their wisdom determine the degree of success the business enjoys.

HILL: And, you believe that a business cannot be successful without the aid of unbiased coordinators known as management?

CARNEGIE: That is the idea. Small, one-man businesses may operate successfully without a coordinator, but the moment any business requires more than one man for its operation, some individual must assume the responsibility of coordinating the factors that affect the business, or it will not succeed.

HILL: Summed up in a few words, what you were saying is that the coordination of individual efforts is essential for success in any business, and the majority of men lack the ability or the inclination to cooperate with others in an efficient, friendly manner?

CARNEGIE: That is precisely what I've been saying, and it is supported by the experience of all able business leaders. The best evidence of its soundness may be found in the well-known fact that while ordinary manual labor is always plentiful, managerial ability always is scarce. This is because men with the temperament, education, experience, and personal inclination to coordinate the efforts of others are scarce. This scarcity accounts for the fact that able managerial ability always commands its own price because here, as elsewhere in the field of economics, the Law of Supply and Demand obtains.

CHAPTER 15

Budgeting of Time and Money

HILL: Mr. Carnegie, you have named the Budgeting of Time as one of the essentials for individual achievement. What methods should one adopt to make the best use of his time?

CARNEGIE: Every successful person plans his life as carefully as a successful businessman plans his business. He begins by adopting a Definite Major Purpose, and he follows through by devoting a definite proportion of his time to attaining the object of that purpose.

Of course, sound health demands balanced physical and mental habits, but successful people have learned how to arrange their work time and their free time so that the free time provides recreation along lines that contribute to and harmonize with the duties they perform during their work time.

HILL: I see the logic of your argument, Mr. Carnegie, but is it not true that a well-rounded life calls for play and recreation? That old saying that all work and no play makes Jack a dull boy seems to be sound.

CARNEGIE: That may be a sound saying, but there are many misconceptions. Speaking for myself, and from my observations of the successful people I have known, I can say that there is no better form of play than that which is associated with the planning and attaining of one's major purpose. It would be a mistake to say that I work hard, for the truth is that I look upon my work as the finest sort of play. So does every other man who is succeeding in the true sense of that term.

A man's work can be a recreation if he does it in a spirit of intense enthusiasm and likes what he is doing. Enthusiasm recreates. An interest in one's work may therefore be recreation.

HILL: But, Mr. Carnegie, wouldn't some people consider it selfish for one to cultivate relationships only with those whom he desired to use?

CARNEGIE: No matter how one may view this habit, it is an essential for personal achievement. Personally, I see nothing selfish about it provided one so relates himself to others that he gives as well as receives, and I have made it clear that I have always followed this practice.

HILL: And what about budgeting your money?

CARNEGIE: The successful man, the one who attains economic success, budgets the use of his money and material assets as carefully as he budgets his time. He sets aside a definite amount of his income, usually determined on a definite percentage of the total for 1) food, clothing, and household expense; 2) life insurance; 3) savings which he puts to work in some form of investments; and 4) charity and recreation.

All four of these items are controlled by a strict budget from which no deviation is made except in cases of emergency. This ensures the saving of a definite percentage of one's income and leads to economic security.

What difference would it make whether a man's income were $100 a month or $1,000 a month if he allowed it all to go for living expenses or spent it for recreation or for any other purpose that did not yield a material return of some sort? I must tell you, however, that the majority of the American people make this very mistake. No matter how much they earn, it all goes out in one way or another because they have no established budget system for saving and properly using a percentage of it. I have known men to receive salary increases only to spend every cent of it on living expenses.

Chapter 16

The Habit of Health

Hill: To maintain a health consciousness requires not only healthy physical habits involving exercise and diet, but one must also think in terms of sound health, not in terms of illness and disease. For whatever the mind dwells upon, the mind brings into existence, whether it be financial success or physical health.

Émile Coué, the great French psychologist, gave the world in one sentence a very simple but practical formula for the maintenance of a health consciousness. "Day by day, in every way, I'm getting better and better." He recommended that this sentence be repeated thousands of times daily until the subconscious section of the mind picked it up, accepted it, and began to carry it out to its logical conclusion in the form of sound health.

The wise ones smiled, not too tolerantly, when they heard of the Coué formula. The not-so-wise accepted it in good faith, put it to work in earnest, and discovered that it produced marvelous results, for it started them on the road toward the development of a health consciousness, and here is the reason why a positive mental attitude is essential for the maintenance of sound health.

CHAPTER 17

Cosmic Habit Force

HILL: Cosmic Habit Force is the particular application of energy with which nature maintains the existing relationship between the atoms of matter, the stars and planets, the seasons of the year, night and day, sickness and health, life and death, and more important to us right now, it is the medium through which all habits and all human relationships are maintained, the medium through which thought is translated into its physical equivalent.

You, of course, know that nature maintains a perfect balance between all the elements of matter and energy throughout the universe. You can see the stars and planets move with perfect precision, each keeping its own place in time and space, year-in and year-out. You can see the seasons of the year come and go with perfect regularity. You can see that night and day follow each other in unending regularity.

You can see that an oak tree grows from an acorn, and a pine grows from the seed of its ancestor. An acorn never produces a pine, nor does a pinecone ever produce an oak, and nothing is ever produced that does not have its antecedents in something else which preceded it.

These are simple facts that anyone can see, but what most people cannot see or understand is the universal law through which nature maintains perfect balance between all matter and energy throughout the universe forcing every living thing to reproduce itself.

We caught a fragmentary glimpse of this great law of nature, which holds our little Earth in its proper position and causes all material objects to be attracted toward the center of the earth when Newton discovered what he called the Law of Gravitation.

And if Newton had gone a few steps beyond where he stopped, perhaps he would have discovered that the same law which holds our little Earth in space and relates it to all the other planets in both time and space, relates human beings to one another in exact conformity with the nature of their own thoughts, he would have discovered that the same force which draws all material things toward the center of this Earth also builds man's thought habits in varying degrees of permanency.

He would have discovered that negative thought habits of whatever nature attract to their creator physical manifestations corresponding to their nature as perfectly as nature germinates the seed of the acorn and develops it into an oak tree.

Also, he would have discovered that positive thoughts reach out through the self-same law and attract physical counterparts of their nature. We are here concerned only with the method by which nature takes a hold on the mind through the operation of the law.

Before we go any further, let us briefly describe an important function of Cosmic Habit Force through which it controls all human relationships and determines whether an individual will be a success or a failure in his chosen occupation. This description can best be made by the statement that nature uses this law as a medium by which every living thing is forced to take on and become a part of the environment in which it lives and moves daily.

We are ruled by habits, all of us. Our habits are fastened upon us by repetition of thought and experience, therefore, we can control our earthly destinies just to the extent that we control our thoughts. It is a profoundly significant fact that over the power of thought a person may have complete control. Everything else is subject to forces outside of one's control. Nature has given man the privilege of controlling his thoughts, but she has also subjected him to the power of Cosmic Habit Force through which his thoughts are made to clothe themselves in their physical likeness and equivalent.

If a man's dominating thoughts are of poverty, the law translates those thoughts into physical terms of misery and want. If a man's dominating thoughts are of opulence, the law transforms them into their physical counterpart. Man builds the pattern through his thoughts, but Cosmic Habit Force works that pattern into its physical likeness and builds it into permanency.

"But, how can a law of nature make something out of nothing," some will ask? It is but natural that any practical person would want to know the exact manner in which, for example, Cosmic Habit Force could transmute thoughts of opulence into material riches or thoughts of poverty into material evidence of poverty. We are happy to raise the question and to answer it.

To begin with, let us recognize the fact that Cosmic Habit Force is silent, unseen, and unfelt and works in complete harmony with all of nature's other forces such as gravitation, electricity, evolution, etc., but it differs from all other natural forces in that it is the sole source of their power and serves as nature's controller through which every form of power and every law of nature must work. It is the master key to the universe, so great in power that it controls every living thing and every atom of matter, the control being carried out through established habit force.

The method by which Cosmic Habit Force converts a positive impulse or mental desire into its physical equivalent is simple. It merely intensifies the desire into a state of mind known as faith, which inspires one to create definite plans for the attainment of whatever is desired, the plans being carried out through whatever natural methods the resourcefulness of the individual can command. Cosmic Habit Force does not undertake to transmute the desires for money directly into bank balances but it does set into motion the mechanism of imagination through which the most easily available means of converting the desire into money is provided in the form of a definite idea, plan, or method of procedure.

This force works no miracles, makes no attempt to create something out of nothing, but it does help an individual, nay it forces him to proceed naturally and logically to convert his thoughts into their physical equivalent by using all the natural media available to him which may serve his purpose. The force works so quietly that the individual, unless he is of a philosophical trend of mind, does not recognize his relationship to what is happening to him.

On one occasion, an idea will present itself to his mind in a form that he calls a hunch, and it will inspire him with such definite faith that he will begin at once to act upon it. His entire being has been changed from a negative to a positive state of mind with the result that related ideas flow into his mind more freely. The plans he creates are more definite, and his words have more influence with other people.

Because he does not understand the source from which his hunch came, he may dismiss the matter and imagine the newly discovered idea or plan with which he achieves success was the creation of his own brain. The hunch is simply a desire that has been given the intensity to enable Cosmic Habit Force to take it over and give it the necessary momentum to convert it into a definite idea or plan of action.

From that point on, the individual must move on his own by using such opportunities, human relationships, and physical conveniences as may be available to him for carrying out his desire. At times, one is inspired with awe by the coincidental combination of favorable circumstances with which he is favored in carrying out his plans such as voluntary cooperation from unexpected sources, some fortunate transaction in business that provides unexpected money, etc., but always these strange and unexplained things happen through perfectly natural procedure similar to daily experiences.

What the individual cannot see or understand is the method by which Cosmic Habit Force gives to one's thoughts that peculiar quality, which gives them the power to surmount all difficulties, overcome all resistances, and achieve seemingly unattainable ends through simple but natural procedure.

That is one secret of nature that is not yet revealed, but neither has she revealed the secret by which she causes a seed of wheat to germinate, grow, and reproduce itself bringing back with it 100 additional grains for good measure.

Cosmic Habit Force guided me through an awe-inspiring maze of experiences before revealing itself to me. All through those years of struggle, there was one definite purpose uppermost in my mind, the burning desire to organize a philosophy with which the average man can become self-determining. Nature had no alternative but that of yielding to me the working principle of Cosmic Habit Force because I unwittingly complied with the law, by persistently seeking the way to its discovery. If I'd known of the existence of the law and of its working principle at the beginning of my research, I could have organized the Philosophy of American Achievement in a much shorter period of time.

It is profoundly significant that the Law of Cosmic Habit Force was revealed after a daily contact of minds through the Mastermind Principle covering a period of almost two years. A major portion of this time was devoted to the analysis of problems which had nothing to do with the voluntary search for the law, but the important thing I wish here to emphasize is the fact that our habit of bringing our minds into rapport for a definite purpose daily actually had the effect of giving us the benefit of Cosmic Habit Force before we knew of the existence of the law.

If your life is not what you wish it to be, you can truthfully say that you drifted into your present, unhappy condition through the irresistible force of Cosmic Habit Force, but you cannot stop there because you shall know presently that time and Definiteness of Purpose backed by Cosmic Habit Force, can give you rebirth no matter who you are or what may be your circumstances.

You may be in prison without friends or money with a life sentence hanging over you, but you can walk through the front gate and back to the outside world of free men if you adapt yourself to this force in the proper manner. How do I know this can be done? Because it has been done before, because your common sense will tell you that it can be done once you understand the working principle and catch the full significance of its relationship to time and Definiteness of Purpose.

You may be suffering with ill health, which prevents you from using your mind. In that event, unless your illness is of a nature that can be cured, you may not be able to order your life just as you would have it, but you can make changes that will give you ample compensation for your trouble in living.

You're going to make another outstanding discovery in connection with this force. You're going to learn that every failure brings with it the seed of an equivalent advantage. You're going to discover beyond any room for doubt that every experience, every circumstance of your life is a potential steppingstone or stumbling block due entirely to the manner in which you react to the circumstance in your own mind.

You are going to discover that your only limitations are those that you set up in your own mind, but more important still, you're going to know that your mind can remove all limitations it establishes. You're going to know that you may be the master of your fate, the captain of your soul because you can control your own thoughts.

You are going to learn that failure is one of nature's methods by which he breaks up the grip of Cosmic Habit Force and releases the mind for a new start. You are going to understand that nature breaks the grip of Cosmic Habit Force on human beings through illness that forces them to rest the organs of the body and the brain. You are going to understand, too, that nature breaks the grip of the law on the people of an entire nation through wars and economic collapses known as depressions, thereby breaking up the monopolies and opportunity and reducing all men to substantially the same level.

I have given you a working knowledge of the relationship between Cosmic Habit Force, drifting, time, and Definiteness of Purpose. I have shown you through illustrations based on actual experience exactly how and why 98 out of every 100 people are failures.

I want you to know that the failures of life become such because they fall into the habit of drifting on all matters affecting their economic life, that Cosmic Habit Force carries them swiftly along in this drifting path until time fastens the habit permanently, after which there can be no escape except through some circumstance of catastrophe which breaks up their established habits and gives them an opportunity to move with Definiteness of Purpose.

I wish you to see that you are where you are and what you are today because of the influences which have reached your mind through your daily environment plus the state of mind in which you have reacted to these influences. I wish you to see and to understand that you can move with purpose and make your environment to order, or you can drift with circumstances and allow your environment to control you.

In both cases, Cosmic Habit Force is an irresistible force. It carries you swiftly toward a definite goal if you have one, and if you are definitely determined to reach that goal, or if you have no goal, it forces you to drift with time and circumstances until you become the victim of every stray wind of chance that crosses your path.

Everything in life worth having has a definite price upon it. There is no such reality as something for nothing. Having had the full advantage of studying Emerson's conclusions on this subject, plus the advantage of analyzing men and women representing the great successes and the outstanding failures, I am prepared to describe why every desirable thing in life has a price that must be paid, but I cannot pass this information onto the person who is not willing to face facts and admit to his own shortcomings. A willingness to look at oneself through unbiased eyes is a part of the price one must pay for the formula that leads to self-determination spiritually, economically, and physically.

Every person who succeeds must make use of some combination of the principles of this philosophy. The power that gives life and action to these principles is Cosmic Habit Force. Whenever any combination of the principles has been used successfully, as far as I have been able to determine by my research and personal experience, the law was unconsciously applied. I mean by this that those who have made successful application of the law have done so by mere chance without recognizing the real source of the power back of their achievements.

Observe the importance of the element of time as an essential factor with which the Principles of Achievement and Cosmic Habit Force becomes related. Cosmic Habit Force is so inexorable that it automatically takes over habits and makes them permanent.

If Cosmic Habit Force crystalizes an impulsive thought of illness and pain into a habit, think how much more quickly it will translate into permanency the pleasant, positive sensations of life. When nature has a message to convey to mankind, she does not release it to those who are indulging in dissipation, nor does she hand it over to those who have been pampered and protected from struggle, but she picks as her torch bearers those who have been seasoned by defeat until they have become self-determining.

This is your destiny. Embark on it.

NAPOLEON HILL was born in 1883 in Wise County, Virginia. He was employed as a secretary, a reporter for a local newspaper, the manager of a coalmine and a lumberyard, and attended law school, before he began working as a journalist for *Bob Taylor's Magazine*, an inspirational and general-interest journal. In 1908, the job led to his interviewing steel magnate Andrew Carnegie. The encounter, Hill said, changed the course of his life. Carnegie believed success could be distilled into principles that anyone could follow, and urged Hill to interview the greatest industrialists, financiers, and inventors of the era to discover these principles. Hill accepted the challenge, which lasted more than twenty years and formed the building block for *Think and Grow Rich*. Hill dedicated the rest of his life to documenting and refining the principles of success. After a long career as an author, magazine publisher, lecturer, and consultant to business leaders, the motivational pioneer died in 1970 in South Carolina.

MITCH HOROWITZ is the PEN Award-winning author of books including *Occult America* and *The Miracle*

Club. A writer-in-residence at the New York Public Library and lecturer-in-residence at the University of Philosophical Research in Los Angeles, Mitch introduces and edits G&D Media's line of Condensed Classics and is the author of the Napoleon Hill Success Course series, including *The Miracle of a Definite Chief Aim* and *The Power of the Master Mind*. Visit him at MitchHorowitz.com.

Printed in the USA
CPSIA information can be obtained
at www.ICGtesting.com
JSHW012042140824
68134JS00033B/3215

9 781722 502133